POURED OUT

A Faith-Based Escape Plan to Crush Debt, Find Your Calling, and Live on the Overflow

Na'Tasha Bull

CONTENTS

INTRODUCTION

Welcome to Your Financial Breakthrough!

You didn't pick up this book by accident. You're here because you're ready for real change, not another feel-good pep talk, not recycled financial advice, and certainly not a lecture filled with fear or statistics. You already know the struggle. What you need now is a strategy that works.

This book is your faith and action blueprint, a step-by-step system designed to pull you out of financial frustration and launch you into lasting freedom. It's not just about numbers; it's about renewing your mindset and partnering with God for transformation. You'll learn to recognize the unique talents and skills God has already placed inside you. These are not random talents; they are resources meant to open doors, create opportunities, and build confidence in what you can do. Once you know what's in your hands, you'll discover how to use it wisely.

You'll learn practical and faith-based strategies to convert your gifts into streams of income.

With purpose-driven income and biblical stewardship, you'll attack debt with clarity and peace. You'll learn to replace fear with faith and watch God multiply what's left in your hands. Your financial freedom is not a dream; it's a decision.

Read this book slowly. Read with expectation. Every chapter holds a key to your next breakthrough. But most importantly, take action.

Knowledge without obedience leads to delay, but faith combined with action leads to destiny. This is your moment to rise, rebuild, and reclaim the life God intended for you.

How To Use This Book

- Read one chapter at a time.
- Complete the worksheet at the end of each chapter.
- At the end of this book, there is a 30-day challenge that will help you implement your plan.

Who am I, and why should you listen to me?

My name is Na'Tasha Bull, and I'm not here to sell you a fantasy. I'm here to tell you the truth. I know what it feels like to be drowning in debt and a believer in the Lord Jesus Christ. Yet my finances did not look like it. My first question was how can I love Christ and I am broke, busted, and disgusted, something is wrong. So, I've been there before COVID-19, during it, and after. I've lived through the stress, the sleepless nights, and the endless cycle of robbing Peter to pay Paul. But I didn't stay there. Through relentless searching, I uncovered simple yet powerful principles that turned my financial situation inside out and right side up. And here's what's crazy, the answers were hidden in plain sight all along.

Now, I'm handing them to you.

If you're tired of feeling like you never have enough. If you're sick of living paycheck to paycheck.

If you're done watching your business or personal finances spiral out of control.

This book is your financial GPS. It will guide you step by step to a place of true debt domination with no fluff, just results.

Get ready. What you're about to learn will not only shift your mindset but completely transform the way you see debt, money, and financial freedom.

You're going to love this book. In fact, don't be surprised if it becomes one of the most impactful reads of your life.

And one day soon, you'll have your own success story to tell.

So, let's get started. The future you've been waiting for is just a few pages away.

CHAPTER 1

Seek your turnaround -Position yourself for God's Shift: Identify Your Financial Turning Point.

In a world where financial security constantly seems like a fairytale, the path from hopelessness to control starts with a step. Imagine the suppressing burden of debt, the constant worry of overdue payments, and the sense of being plunged into a loop of poor financial choices. The fascinating and mind-blowing news within these challenges is that a potent chance for change still exists.

What I am about to share will reveal the simplest principles that have always been at your fingertips. You will be amazed when you see how one widow transformed her financial story by simply following instructions. She turned her situation from bleak to bright with an uncomplicated, hands-on strategy, making her financial freedom a dream come through.

If you are in debt, you may not have mastered money management skills. However, as you read this content, you will be significantly closer to financial mastery, where managing money becomes second nature, than you were before. Stack the deck in your favor.

To "stack the deck" means arranging things in a way that gives you an advantage. It's about positioning yourself strategically so that success becomes more attainable. It can also mean arranging a deck of cards (or other objects) in such a way that it gives you an unfair advantage because you know the order before the hidden side is revealed.

The Bible itself contains principles that, when applied, provide a profound and earnest advantage in life, including financial wisdom and literacy. The entire Bible is a series of stacks that give those who know it "practically an unfair" advantage over those who don't. My job is to learn to take advantage of the many opportunities laid out. Your job is to learn to take advantage of these opportunities as well.

Let's explore a powerful story from the Bible that demonstrates these principles in action:

2 Kings 4:1-3 "A widow, whose husband was part of a group of prophets, approached Elisha, saying, 'My husband, your servant, has died. You know he was devoted to the Lord, but he left debt behind. Now, the creditors are coming to take my two sons as payment

Elisha responded, "What do you want me to do? Tell me, what do you have in your house?" Surprised by his question, she replied, "I have nothing... except a small jar of oil."

Elisha then instructed, "Go borrow empty containers from your neighbors, get as many as you can. Then, go inside, shut the door behind you and your sons, and start pouring the oil into the containers. Set each one aside when it is full."

She followed his instructions. 2 Kings 4:6 "When all the containers were filled, she asked her son for another, but he said, 'There are no more containers.' At that moment, the oil remained. She returned to Elisha, and he told her, 'Go sell the oil, pay off your debts, and you and your sons can live on what's left."

At first, Elisha's response may seem indifferent. The woman had lost her husband, was about to lose her sons, and desperately sought help. Yet, instead of immediately offering money, Elisha redirected her focus to personal responsibility.

This widow and her husband had accumulated debt, and she was looking for someone to fix it. But Elisha's wisdom teaches us an essential financial lesson: Expect more from yourself than from others. External help is valuable, but true financial change starts with self-examination and resourcefulness. 2 Kings 4:2 Then he said, 'Tell me, what do you have in your house?' When he said, "tell me," here's what he was really saying: if you can't fix this problem, you have to learn how to express yourself. What do I mean by expressing yourself? He was basically saying, "You've told me about the problem, and I understand it completely. Your husband died. I get it. They're about to take your kids. I get that too. So, in response to everything happening around you, what actions have you taken? Examine yourself!

He acknowledged Self-expression while teaching self-examination. See, here's what Elisha knew, which this woman hadn't figured out yet: Instead of the woman coming to him to have a sit-down and ask for money, she should have first taken some time to herself to say, 'What do I already have that I can sell to make money?' However, I do personally understand the widow, because it's almost like a cultural engraving on our hearts, through the years, that when we get ourselves into trouble, it is best to go around and see who can get us out of what we got ourselves into.

We've learned from our family members, our teachers, our preachers, our spouses, the people we care about, and even our siblings. We've learned that talking about the problem is somehow the thing to do when we have problems. Hence, the popular phrase, "a problem shared is half solved." I submit to you that talking about the problem only makes it worse. Elisha said, "Tell me, what do you have in the house?" He was asking, "What solutions have you come up with?"

To truly overcome challenges, we must first recognize our own role in creating or perpetuating them. We must be self-aware. I know Elisha's words might have sounded a bit tough to the woman, but the reality is that the Scripture says, "Faithful are the wounds of a friend, but the kisses of an enemy are deceitful" (Proverbs 27:6). I'd rather give you help that hurts you. What do I mean by that? I would rather hurt you to help you. I clearly agree with Elisha on this. I would rather hurt you to help you than help you to harm you. Sometimes, when people fix your problems too fast, you don't learn how to fix them yourself. It's usually a quick-fix fire brigade approach that leaves you without improvement. Hopefully, you're picking up what I'm putting down.

Steps to Financial Transformation

Identify Your Gifts: What are your natural talents? What do you do effortlessly? Brainstorm on the things you do so well without stress that they almost feel second nature. Maybe you have a gift for creativity, painting, writing, or crafting stories that captivate others. Perhaps you're an analytical thinker - someone who can break down complex problems and see solutions and opportunities in blind spots. Maybe your strength lies in how you connect with people, making them feel heard, valued, and understood.

Whatever they are, these unique gifts and talents hold the key to unlocking many opportunities in your life. Sadly, sometimes, we overlook them because they come so naturally that we assume they aren't special. We dismiss them as just "how we are."

I know this all too well. For years, I never realized that the gift of my ability to talk was my golden ticket to financial freedom. While growing up, I constantly got in trouble for talking too much. I bet you know exactly what I'm talking about!) Teachers would call my name, give me that weird look, and say, 'Do you ever stop talking?' Friends and family would tease me, asking, "Do you even breathe between sentences?"

For the longest time, I thought my talkative nature was just a personality trait, something I couldn't help but do. Over time, I realized that it was more than that. I wasn't just talking; I was engaging, inspiring, and helping people see new perspectives. I could take any topic and casually transform it into an insightful, thought-provoking conversation.

It wasn't until later in life that I realized this wasn't just "who I was," it was a powerful gift. A tool, and like any tool, it needed to be sharpened and directed towards a purpose.

Talking, something I have been doing all my life, became the foundation for my career, my success, and my financial freedom. The treasure I was searching for was already deposited inside me. I just needed the right guidance to unlock its full potential. Funnily enough, this holds true for you, too.

What's already inside of you that you haven't fully tapped into? What comes so naturally that you barely even recognize it as a gift? Take a moment to reflect. Your talent and gift have been with you all along. It's time to look within and start using them.

Market Research

How are others making money with skills similar to yours? Where can you add value?

The truth is that people are turning their natural gifts into thriving businesses every day. Whether it's speaking, reading, writing, coaching, designing, problem-solving, or creating, there are endless ways to monetize what comes naturally to you. Find out how other people are using similar gifts and talents, add a little bit of fine-tuning or tweaking, identify market gaps, and position yourself strategically.

That's exactly what I did.

Once I realized that talking was something I had been doing effortlessly, my entire life became my gift. I started researching. I looked at social media, online platforms, and community discussions. I asked myself: Who needs this skill? Where can I be more relevant?

Then, it hit me: Children, teenagers, young adults, parents, and just people.

I kid you not, I don't have a college degree, a fancy certification, or anything remotely official but I have solid experience, passion, and a natural ability to communicate in ways that resonate.

I started making cool money doing what had always come naturally to me. Talking to kids about social skills, teaching them the importance of kindness, and helping them understand why respecting and honoring their parents matters. In addition, I started offering solutions to parents struggling with discipline, communication, and raising confident, well-mannered children.

For years, I had been doing this for free, offering advice, guiding kids, and helping parents navigate the challenges of raising children, and just knowing how to be the best parent they could be. Advising on self-care, relationships, and just being who God says you are. I just never realized that this was a marketable skill. I never knew this was one of my money-makers.

Identifying and understanding your audience. Who needs what you naturally offer? Who would benefit from your skills, knowledge, or expertise? There are lots of people looking for what you carry and offer. You need to identify them. Once you discover where your talents align with a real need, you can transform what you love into what you do and what you do into money.

For me, nothing is more fulfilling than spending time with children and their parents. Helping them grow, ministering to those struggling with living this life, and making a real impact while earning a great income.

So, what about you?

Develop Your Skills

When you've identified your talents and gifts, you take the bold step of refining them. Though raw gift and talent are valuable and can take you miles ahead in life, sharpening them through education, practice, and exposure can take you from miles to a world of limitless opportunities and conversions.

It is highly important to invest time in improving or diversifying your skills through online courses, workshops, mentorship, and hands-on practice. The more you grow, the more value you can offer, the more relevant you become, and the more opportunities will come your way.

That's exactly what I did.

When I discovered that speaking and teaching people was my gift, I knew I couldn't rely on raw talent alone. I wanted to do and be better. I wanted to be more effective. So, I took action.

I enrolled in leadership courses at a community college to strengthen my ability to guide and influence. I joined groups that aligned with my passion, places where I could learn from those who had already mastered the art of teaching children and adults in today's world.

I didn't stop there.

I invested in coaching courses, attended seminars both online and in person, and studied the techniques of top speakers. I learned how to present myself with confidence, how to connect with an audience, and, most importantly, how to say the right things at the right time.

And, of course, I devoured books about public speaking, communication, and personal development. Every piece of knowledge I gained added another layer to my ability to serve, teach, and inspire. Now, I submit this challenge to you.

Make a list

Write down the things you are naturally good at, the things that come effortlessly, the skills you've been using all your life to help others. What problems have you been solving for people without even realizing it? This is where your fulfillment lies. This is where your potential to serve, create, and monetize truly begins.

The greatest investment you can ever make is in yourself, because when you commit to growth, your talents evolve, your confidence rises, and your impact expands. So, what will you do today to hone your gifts?

Build a Personal Brand

In today's world, having an online presence isn't a choice; it's a necessity. Whether you love it or not, social media is here to stay. Platforms like Facebook, TikTok, Instagram, and YouTube have changed the dynamics, allowing people to connect, share their expertise, and build successful businesses all within the comfort of their homes.

Brainstorm over that for a moment.

You no longer need a physical store, a mind-boggling budget, or a marketing team to reach your audience. All you need is a phone, an internet connection, and the willingness to put yourself out there. A click of a button can showcase your talents, build a following, and start making money.

If you're like me and love talking to people, video content can be a powerful way to engage your audience. YouTube, TikTok, Instagram Reels: these platforms give you direct access to the people who need what you offer. At first, it might feel a little scary. Hitting that "record" button can make your heart race. But let me tell you this: after a few videos, you'll feel like a pro. Confidence comes with practice. Video isn't the only way to build your brand.

Another effective tool is building a website. A personal website or portfolio serves as your digital storefront, a space where you control the narrative, showcase your services or products, and establish credibility. Whether you're offering coaching, selling products, or providing a service, your website is a place where potential clients can learn more about you and take action.

Your brand is essentially a mirror, reflecting your true self: your unique talents, values, and message. The more authentic you are, the stronger the connection you'll create with your audience.

So, where will you start?

Will you kick off with a going live on social media, recording your first video, setting up your website, or starting your podcast? Whatever path you choose, remember that your voice, your skills, and your message deserve to be heard. The world is waiting for what you have to offer.

Network Strategically

Success isn't a solo journey; it's built on relationships, collaboration, teamwork, and learning from those who have walked the path before you. Surrounding yourself with like-minded individuals and professionals in your field can open doors you never even knew existed. Opportunities, collaborations, and mentorship all stem from the connections you make. The right people will challenge you, inspire you, and push you to grow beyond your comfort zone.

As I mentioned earlier, you need to be part of a group that aligns with your gifts. Whether it's a mastermind group, a professional network, or an online community, immersing yourself in an environment where others share your passion will keep you motivated and on track.

Mentorship.

A mentor is someone who has already been where you're trying to go. They've faced challenges, made mistakes, and figured out the strategies for success. Having a mentor can fast-track your progress by giving you insight, advice, and guidance that would otherwise take years to learn on your own. Having a mentor makes the journey even smoother and hassle-free

So, ask yourself:

- Who are the people in your field that you admire?
- Where do they gather online, in groups, at events?
- How can you start connecting with them today?

Don't be afraid to reach out, ask questions, and build genuine relationships. Networking isn't about taking; it's about giving value, supporting others, and growing together.

Success leaves clues. Surround yourself with people who inspire you, and before long, you'll find yourself stepping into the success you were meant for, and this changes everything about your perception of life.

Offer Services or Products

Your gifts were never intended to remain unnoticed. They are intended to be shared, to help others, and yes, to make you money.

The secret is to figure out how to package your skills so that others can benefit from them.

There are countless ways to monetize your natural abilities. Whether through consulting, coaching, tutoring, freelancing, or selling handmade crafts, digital products, or online courses, the possibilities are endless. The question is: How will you use your gifts to serve others?

Start by brainstorming:

- **Are you a natural teacher?** Consider tutoring, coaching, or creating educational content.
- **Do you have a creative gift?** Sell handmade crafts, digital designs, or artwork.
- **Are you great at problem-solving?** Offer consulting services to those who need your expertise.
- **Do you have a way with words?** Start a blog, write books, or create engaging social media content.

Your talents are valuable, but they need structure to become profitable. Think about what you already do naturally, what people often come to you for advice or help with. That is where your business or side hustle can begin.

Making money from your gifts is only one aspect of monetizing them; another is making a difference. It's about creating a fulfilling life for yourself and using what you've been given to make someone else's life better. So, take the first step, grab a notebook, start brainstorming, and map out how you can turn your unique talents into a thriving business or side income. The world is waiting for what you have to offer.

Seek Feedback and Adapt

Growth is a continuous process, and one of the most powerful ways to improve is by seeking feedback. Whether you're offering a service, selling a product, or building a brand, constructive criticism is invaluable. It helps you refine your skills, enhance your offerings, and stay relevant in an ever-changing world.

Be open to feedback

It's easy to take criticism personally, but instead of seeing it as a setback, view it as a tool for growth. The most successful people in any industry are those who listen, learn, and adapt. Never fall into the trap of thinking you've "arrived" and no longer need improvement. The moment you stop learning is the moment you stop growing.

Stay informed and adaptable.

We live in a digital age where consumer demands, technology, and trends are ever-changing. What was effective yesterday might not be so tomorrow. This implies that you need to keep up to date, whether it's through continuing education, news from the industry, or direct audience feedback. Ask yourself:

- What do my customers or clients frequently ask for?
- Where can I improve my service or product?
- What's happening in my industry that I need to be aware of?

The best way to stay in demand is to remain flexible. Be willing to tweak, adjust, and innovate. If you listen, learn, and implement changes based on what you discover, you won't just stay relevant, you'll stay ahead.

So, embrace feedback. Seek it out. Use it as fuel for growth. Because the more you adapt, the stronger and more successful you'll become. One of the biggest barriers to financial success is the belief that you have nothing valuable to offer. Many people think, "I'm just me," but history proves otherwise:

- Justin Bieber "just sang" on YouTube and built a global career.
- Rachel Ray "just cooked" and became a culinary icon.
- Oprah Winfrey "just talked" and became a media mogul.
- Martha Stewart "just cooked, cleaned, and sewed" and built a billion-dollar empire.

I'm here to let you know that one of your biggest problems is that you haven't taken inventory of your gifts. Do you know why?

Because, like so many other people, you suffer from the world's most prolific business disease. What's that called? I'm just meitis—inflammation of the "I'm just me" gland. Your "I'm just me" gland is so swollen and so inflamed that you value everybody else's gifts but your own. You know I'm telling the truth. "Man, if I could just sing like so-and-so," or "If I could just write poetry like them," or "If I could just cook like them," or "If I could just talk like them," or "If I could just teach like them." You're looking at their gifts, wishing you had theirs, and they're looking at you, wishing they had yours.

Financial transformation requires deliberate action rather than chance. You cannot find if you do not seek. Find a little, seek a little. Find a lot by searching a lot. The path from poverty to prosperity is frequently a difficult but motivating one that requires a number of qualities, including fortitude and a modicum of faith. Therefore, utilizing your innate abilities and gifts to pursue a financial turnaround calls for a calculated approach. Your financial breakthrough may be closer than you think. The answers are within your reach. Now, go and find them.

CHAPTER 1 WORKSHEET: IDENTIFY YOUR FINANCIAL TURNING POINT

Section 1: Your Current Reality Check-Get your pen, and let's start writing the vision on paper

1. What financial situation are you currently facing? (Be honest and specific.)

____

____

____

Examples: debt amount, overdue bills, emotional stress, patterns you've noticed.

2. What emotions do you feel when you think about your finances?

(Check all that apply)

☐ Overwhelmed

☐ Afraid

- ☐ Embarrassed
- ☐ Determined
- ☐ Hopeful
- ☐ Confused
- ☐ Motivated
- ☐ Other: ____________________

3. What part of your situation feels "out of control"?

____

____

____

Section 2: "What Do You Have in Your House?" Inventory

Inspired by Elisha's question to the widow (2 Kings 4):

4. List every resource, possession, skill, or tool you currently have that could be useful.

Think: time, talents, items, connections, experience, hobbies.

____

____

____

____

5. Which of these have you overlooked or underestimated? Why?

____

____

____

Section 3: Identify Your God-Given Gifts

6. What comes naturally to you? What do people often praise you for?

____

____

7. What activities do you do effortlessly without needing to be paid, pushed, or prompted?

____

____

8. Write one gift you now recognize as a financial opportunity:

____

____

Section 4: "I'm Just Me-itis" Reflection

9. Where have you devalued your gifts?

Finish this sentence:

"I always thought I was just someone who ."

____

____

10. Who do you admire for their talent, and what similar talent do YOU actually possess?

____

____

____

Section 5: Market Research Starter

11. List 3 people who use a gift similar to yours to earn money.

(Example: speakers, tutors, stylists, cooks, writers, creators, coaches.)

12. What gap or unmet need do you notice that YOU could fill?

Section 6: Skill Development Plan

13. What skill do you want to sharpen or develop further?

14. What specific action will you take this month to grow in that skill?

(Check one or add your own)

☐ Enroll in a course

☐ Read a book

☐ Watch tutorials

☐ Attend a workshop

☐ Practice daily

☐ Get a mentor

☐ Join a group

☐ Other:

Section 7: Build Your Personal Brand

15. Which platform will you use to start sharing your gift?

(Check all that apply)

☐ YouTube

☐ TikTok

☐ Instagram

☐ Facebook

☐ Podcast

☐ Website

☐ Blog

☐ Other: ____________________________________

16. What is your first piece of content or message going to be about?

____

____

____

Section 8: Networking Strategy

17. List 3 groups, communities, or people you want to connect with.

____

____

____

18. What value can YOU offer to others in your network?

____

____

____

Section 9: Monetizing Your Gifts

19. Which service, product, or offer could you start with?

(Choose one to begin with!)

☐ Coaching

- ☐ Consulting
- ☐ Tutoring
- ☐ Online course
- ☐ Handmade product
- ☐ Digital product (printable, worksheets, templates)
- ☐ Speaking
- ☐ Writing
- ☐ Mentoring
- ☐ Babysitting/child engagement
- ☐ Other: ______________________________

20. What problem will your offer help people solve?

____

____

____

Section 10: Feedback & Adaptation

21. Who can you ask for honest feedback about your gift or offer?

____

____

____

22. What part of your idea needs improvement or clarity?

____

____

____

Section 11: Your Personal Turning Point Declaration

23. Write a clear, powerful commitment statement based on what you learned. (Example: "I commit to using my God-given gift of teaching to generate income, build confidence, and serve others this year.")

____

____

____

BONUS: PRAYER OF ALIGNMENT

24. Write a short prayer asking God for clarity, courage, and direction for your financial shift. Just write like you, no special words or phrases, be your authentic self.

Example: God, this is Na'Tasha, and I read this book and it has a lot of things in it that have got me thinking about……. and end your prayer IN JESUS' NAME!

____

____

____

____

CHAPTER 2

Trusting the Process – Trade Fear for Faith: Let Go So God Can Lead

Do you know what the word “submit” truly means?

It means to place yourself under the authority of another. To humble yourself, listen, and be willing to learn. Submission is not about weakness; it’s about positioning yourself for growth and breakthrough.

When the widow approached the prophet Elisha, she came to him in desperation, crying out for help. What did he do? His response to the average person would have been offensive, but here’s the key: she didn’t get offended; she got ready. Let me say that again: She didn’t get offended; she got ready.

Some people are overly sensitive. They wear their emotions openly and are very quick to take offense when challenged. If you fall into this category. Listen closely: you need to get over yourself. You need to stop being so fragile. Toughen up, buttercup. Growth doesn’t happen in comfort zones, and if you’re easily offended by correction or guidance, you’ll miss the very wisdom that could change your life.

The widow approached Elisha feeling distressed, and instead of comforting her feelings, he jolted her awake. It's as if he were shouting, Wake up! Pay attention! Guess what? She did. Instead of becoming defensive, she leaned in and listened. She realized that the solution to her problem was in following his guidance, even if it seemed unusual and uncomfortable.

Now, let's analyze her reality:

1. Her first problem? Death. She had lost her husband.
2. Her second problem? Debt. Her family owed money they couldn't repay.
3. Her third problem? Doubt. Her children were about to be taken from her, and she felt helpless.

Death. Debt. Doubt.

Yet, despite her overwhelming circumstances, she chose faith over offense and obedience over pride. That decision transformed everything.

Now, ask yourself:

Are you willing to submit to someone who knows more than you?

Can you handle corrections without getting defensive?

Will you take action even when the instructions seem unconventional?

The difference between staying stuck and stepping into your new beginning is often your ability to submit to wise counsel and apply what you've learned. The widow did. Did Elisha tell the widow, "Go get out of debt. Go pay off all your credit cards"? No, that's not what he said. Instead, he started with a series of questions. And then, when He finally gave her instructions, the very first thing he told her to do was just two words: "Go borrow." Can you imagine how crazy that must have sounded to a woman already drowning in debt? Her children were on the verge of being taken from her because she couldn't repay what she owed, and now the prophet was telling her to go borrow more?

If I were her, I might have said, Didn't you just hear what I said? I already can't pay back what I owe, and now you're telling me to borrow again? But here's the truth: Over 90 percent of good coaching, regardless of the field, is counterintuitive. The best advice rarely makes sense at first. It often goes against everything we've been conditioned to believe.

This reminds me of something my mentor once told me about coaching his sons in basketball. "I wasn't the best basketball coach, but I was a good coach when it came to winning. I didn't know much about the game, but I did know this: practice has to be harder than the game itself. So, here's what we did: We ran. We ran laps. We did suicides. Then we shot some basketball. Then we ran more laps.

More suicides. More running. More suicides. And guess what? More running. More suicides.

The boys would look at me like, 'Coach, I'm going to die.' And I'd tell them, Good. Until you die, keep running. We were the worst team in our conference. But then, something happened. The district champs, the best team, invited us to play them for their homecoming game. Guess what? We. Beat. Them. For the first time in history, our team mopped them up. My oldest son dropped 53 points on them as a 10th grader. Why? Because the team with the most energy in the first Quarter isn't the team that wins. The team with the most energy in the fourth quarter is the one that wins.

We may not have been better than them, but we refused to run out of gas before they did."

That's how success works. It doesn't always make sense. Sometimes, the strategy that leads to your breakthrough is the very thing that seems like the worst idea in the moment. The widow trusted Elisha's words even when they didn't make sense. The team trusted their coach even when the training felt unbearable. In both cases, victory came to those who stayed in the game and followed the process.

When Elisha indirectly told the widow, "Well, until you die, keep running", it might have sounded heartless at first, right? But that's only until you get to the fourth quarter, and then you find yourself running circles around the enemy, the opposition. The widow's situation seemed hopeless. She was drowning in debt, and her children were about to be taken from her, but Elisha wasn't heartless. He was guiding her to the breakthrough she needed. He was showing her the power of persistence and obedience, even when things didn't make sense. Elisha didn't tell her to simply stop, pay off her debt, and wait for things to change. No, he told her something far more powerful. He indirectly said, "I know debt is your problem, but I serve a God who can use your problem to solve your problem.

Come here and observe the first principle: Submit to a teacher." In that moment, Elisha wasn't just offering advice; he was providing a strategy. And that strategy began with something that must have sounded completely absurd: "Go borrow." He didn't just say, "Go borrow a little." He told her to borrow as much as possible.

Now, many of us have heard the popular advice: "Get out of debt. Be debt-free." While becoming debt-free is a noble goal, it's not always the first step on the path to true financial freedom. Here's the thing: being debt-free is fine. It's good, even, but it's not necessarily the strategy that wealth- building works with. For those of you thinking, "Well, once I pay off my debt, then I'll focus on building wealth," that's okay if that's your plan. Let me be real with you, that's not how wealthy people think. That's not how they got rich.

Let me explain: I'm willing to wager that the majority of small business owners you speak with while driving through your town will admit that they didn't launch their companies from the ground up. They didn't hesitate to start with borrowed funds. Why? God, in His wisdom, created debt as a tool for people to use to change their circumstances when used wisely. You see, Elisha didn't just say, "Go borrow." He told the widow, "Go borrow empty containers from your neighbors." Not a little. He didn't say borrow just enough to get by. He said, "Go borrow from everyone who will lend to you." He was pushing her to stretch beyond her comfort zone. He was urging her to take bold action.

Does this sound crazy to you? It does to most people. But you know what? It's crazy good. Elisha knew exactly what he was doing; he was guiding her to a financial breakthrough. She did what seemed outlandish. She followed Elisha's instructions and borrowed containers from her neighbors. And you know what happened? The oil didn't stop pouring until there were no more containers left.

Now, let's pause and reflect. Why are you borrowing money? Are you borrowing for a true investment? To invest in yourself, your education, or the business you're about to launch? Or are you borrowing just to get by? When it comes to becoming financially free, you need to recognize this: borrowing isn't the same as living off debt. There is such a thing as "good debt," or debt that is strategically employed for expansion. Good debt is, for instance, when you are ready to start your own business, make educational investments, or fund a project that will bring in money. To invest in your future, you are taking out a loan.

In this moment, you're not borrowing just to pay off old debts. You're borrowing with a purpose. You're using borrowed funds to elevate yourself, not just to survive, but to thrive. This shift in mindset is what separates those who are financially stuck from those who are moving toward financial freedom. And while you might not be able to borrow money from your neighbors or family anymore, perhaps, because they don't believe in your vision or they can't see the potential in your creativity, that's okay. You'll tap into a new source of funding. It could be through investors, loans for your business, or other financial institutions that recognize your potential. This is a shift in your income world. You are no longer just working for a paycheck. You are becoming the service or the product, and when you invest in your gifts, talents, and vision, the return on the investment will be much greater than anything you could have imagined.

This is the true financial freedom, one where you don't just get out of debt, but you build wealth with intention. It's time to step into your power and use your financial resources wisely, not just to survive, but to thrive.

Let me ask you this: Think about someone like Martha Stewart. Is it her cooking and cleaning that's the true value, or is it her? Right, she is the value. If she doesn't cook, if she doesn't clean, no value is created, but because she is in demand, she doesn't rely on a job to pay her bills. She does what has always come naturally to her, solving people's cooking and cleaning problems. Whenever she needs more money, all she has to do is turn on her camera and sell her treasure again and again, and millions of people are always ready to watch.

This is exactly what happens when you understand your gifts and start working in your purpose. Like Martha, you don't need a "job." You're simply adding value to the world through your talents, and that value turns into financial freedom. Back to our story. Did you notice that the widow ran out of containers before she ran out of oil? She borrowed just enough to set her family free, but she still didn't borrow enough containers. She said to her son, "Bring me another container," but he replied, "There are no more." That was when the oil stopped flowing. The miracle ended, not because the oil ran out, but because there were no more containers to fill.

That's what you call overflow, she had more than enough to meet her needs and still have oil left over after all her debt was paid. The lesson here is powerful. When you align yourself with your purpose, when you act in faith and obedience, God's provision will not only meet your needs but will overflow into abundance.

I want to point out something easy to overlook. The teacher in this story doesn't have to be me, or my mentor, or anyone you know. The teacher could be anyone who has the wisdom and experience to guide you toward your financial freedom. The truth is that you would already be free of financial servitude if you could teach yourself how to do so. Who is your teacher, then? Consider it. There are more teachers than just the people you meet in class. Books, podcasts, internet videos, and even a coach who has been where you want to go can all offer them. You can alter your circumstances if you can access their knowledge.

But here's the thing: do your research. Don't jump into something without a clear direction. Search out free information. Head to social media and see what others in your niche are saying. Visit the library and read up on your gifts. As you do this, you'll begin to discover who's been successful in the area you're pursuing. Tap into their materials, learn how they crafted their brand, and use their strategies as inspiration. There are so many free resources out there, YouTube, podcasts, and free webinars. You can even go to your local bank for advice on your idea and how other businesses are doing financially. Don't be afraid to seek guidance from professionals who have been where you're trying to go. The widow's faith in Elisha's words and her obedience to his instructions led to her miraculous provision. The key takeaway here is that faith and community support can lead to a breakthrough, especially during difficult times.

The widow's story is more than just a lesson in finances; it's about the importance of faith, obedience, and trusting in God's ability to provide in abundance. Her faith in Elisha's words opened the door to the miraculous, and her obedience created the space for God to work. This is a powerful reminder: your financial freedom isn't just about you. It's about being part of a community that supports you, believes in you, and encourages you to keep going. Surround yourself with people who elevate your vision, and avoid those who diminish it.

Find your teacher, someone who can show you the way. Trust in what they know. Trust in what they believe. Trust that their experience can help you see things you may not be able to see yet. If you do this, I promise you, you will win. You will not just survive; you will thrive.

Every effort you put forth is moving you closer to the freedom you desire. Your financial future holds unlimited potential, but only if you stay optimistic, stay open, and stay focused. A good teacher will help you focus on what can be, not what is. They will encourage you to see opportunities, set and smash new goals, and embrace new experiences while introducing you to a wider audience.

I'm sure the widow's view of herself grew dramatically during this process. When Elisha asked her, "What do you have in your house?" she didn't hesitate. She recognized that even in her scarcity, there was something of value in her. And as she followed Elisha's instructions, she experienced growth not only financially but spiritually. She knew that with faith, all things are possible.

This is the same for you. As you commit to learning, growing, and following the right guidance, you will begin to realize that your potential is limitless. You have a gift inside of you that the world needs. It's time to find the teacher who will lead you into the financial Promised Land, a place of abundance and provision, a place where you live intentionally and purposefully.

Allow yourself to be receptive to your teacher's wisdom. Allow their insight to lead you to the financial independence you are due. And as you develop, learn, and have faith in the process, you'll not only improve your financial status but also change your life in ways you never would have thought possible. Creating a meaningful, enriching relationship with a teacher, someone who believes in you and your dreams, is a game-changer. Seek out mentors who will show you how to apply wisdom to your situation, someone who can walk with you through the process. With the right guidance, you will learn how to use your unique gifts to create value in the world. You will understand how to tap into the overflow that God has for you, and you'll never look at your gifts the same way again.

The widow's story teaches us that we can move from scarcity to abundance. And it's not about just making do, it's about thriving, living in overflow. The journey starts with a willingness to learn, to trust, and to follow the right teacher, and it ends in financial freedom that reflects the faith and obedience you've shown along the way.

CHAPTER 2 WORKSHEET: TRUSTING THE PROCESS— FROM OFFENDED TO READY

She didn't get offended; she got ready.

Section 1: What Does "Submit" Mean To You? In your own words, what does the word submit mean?

____

____

____

When you hear the phrase "place yourself under the authority of another", what feelings rise in you?

(Check all that apply.)

☐ Resistance

☐ Fear

☐ Relief

☐ Trust

☐ Curiosity

☐ Skepticism

☐ Other:

On a scale from 1–10, how willing are you (right now) to submit to a teacher, mentor, or coach who knows more than you in the area of finances?

Circle one:

1 2 3 4 5 6 7 8 9 10

(Not willing at all) (Completely willing)

What holds you back from fully submitting to wise counsel?

____

____

____

Section 2: Are You Easily Offended or Getting Ready?

Think of the last time someone corrected you or challenged your thinking about money, decisions, or life.

What did they say?

____

____

How did you react at first?

☐ I got defensive

☐ I got quiet and shut down

☐ I ignored them

☐ I thought about it later

☐ I leaned in and listened

☐ Other: ______________________________

Finish this sentence honestly:

"When someone corrects me, my first reaction usually is to…"

____

____

What would it look like for you to "not get offended, but get ready" the next time someone gives you tough truth?

Write one practical response you can choose instead of offense.

____

____

____

Section 3: Death, Debt, Doubt: Your Reality Check

The widow faced Death, Debt, and Doubt. These three still show up today in different forms. In your current life, how do each of these shows up (if at all)?

Death (loss, endings, grief, something that "died" – a dream, job, relationship, etc.):

____

____

____

Debt (financial debt, emotional debt, time debt, feeling "behind"):

____

____

Doubt (fear, uncertainty, unbelief, second-guessing yourself or God):

____

____

Which of these three feels strongest in your life right now?

☐ Death ☐ Debt ☐ Doubt

Why?

____

____

____

What would choosing faith over offense and obedience over pride look like in your current situation?

Section 4: Counterintuitive Instructions

"Over 90% of good coaching is counterintuitive."

Describe a time when someone gave you advice that didn't make sense at first, but later you realized it was good for you.

____

____

____

When God (or a mentor) gives you instructions that feel "crazy" or uncomfortable, which response feels most like you?

☐ I ignore it until it feels logical

☐ I delay and overthink

☐ I partially obey

☐ I obey even if it doesn't make sense

☐ It depends on how much it stretches me

Write a short statement you can tell yourself when God's guidance or coaching feels uncomfortable:

"When the instruction doesn't make sense, I will…"

____

____

____

Section 5: Borrowing With Purpose vs. Living Off Debt

Right now, are you mostly:

☐ Using debt just to survive (stay afloat)

☐ Using debt strategically to grow (invest, build, learn)

☐ Avoiding all debt out of fear

☐ Not sure what I'm doing with debt

Make two lists:

A. Debts that drain me (no growth, just survival):

____

____

____

B. Potential "good debt" I could use strategically (education, business, tools, training):

____

____

____

Is there one area where a wise, purposeful investment (even if borrowed) could move you toward financial freedom instead of just helping you stay stuck?

____

____

____

Section 6: Who Is Your Teacher?

"If you could teach yourself how to break free from financial bondage, you'd already be there."

List 3 potential teachers/mentors in your life (they can be people, books, courses, pastors, coaches, or online voices):

Name/Source: ____________________________________

How they can help me: ______________________________

Name/Source: ____________________________________

How they can help me: ______________________________

Name/Source: ____________________________________

How they can help me: ______________________________

Which one will you intentionally submit to in this next season (choose 1 to start)? Teacher/Resource: ____________________

How I will submit (listen, learn, show up, follow through):

____

What specific action step will you take in the next 7 days to learn from this teacher? (Example: subscribe, schedule a call, join a class, buy their book, watch their videos.)

____

____

____

Section 7: Your "Containers" and Capacity for Overflow

The oil only stopped when there were no more containers.

What are your current "containers," places where God can pour increase into your life? (Examples: your business idea, a side hustle, a skill, a platform, a service.)

Container 1: ______________________________

Container 2: ______________________________

Container 3: ______________________________

Where are you limiting God's flow by bringing too few "containers" (low expectations, small goals, no plan, no offers)?

____

____

____

Write one bold way you can "borrow more containers" expand your capacity for more (more offers, more clients, more learning, more action).

____

____

____

Section 8: OFFENDED vs READY: Self-Check

Check the statements that sound like the old you (offended):

☐ "They're being too hard on me."

☐ "They don't understand my situation."

☐ "I shouldn't have to do all that."

☐ "That's just not my personality."

☐ "If it were God, it would be easier."

Now check the statements that describe the new you (ready):

☐ "This correction is uncomfortable, but it's for my growth."

☐ "I'm willing to be stretched."

☐ "I will follow the process, even when it doesn't make sense yet."

☐ "I choose faith over offense and obedience over pride."

☐ "I'd rather be helped than coddled."

Choose one old statement you will retire and rewrite it as a new declaration:

Old: ____

New: ____

Section 9: Prayer & Declaration of Submission

Write a short prayer of submission to God, inviting Him to guide you to the right teacher and give you the courage not to be offended, but to be ready:

____

____

____

Now write your Declaration of Readiness:

“Today, I choose to submit to wise counsel. I will not be easily offended. I will follow godly instruction, even when it doesn’t make sense at first, because I believe God can use my obedience to bring me into overflow.”

Sign & date it as a personal covenant:

Signature: ____

Date: ____

CHAPTER 3

The Oil in Your House - Unearthing the Gifts Within: Discover What God Planted in You

Maybe the reason it's easier for us to see the value in others than to recognize our own worth is that the one person we can't see with our own eyes is ourselves. This mindset often arises from negative self-perception, comparisons to others, or past experiences that have led us to undervalue what we bring to the table.

When we believe we lack intrinsic value, it creates a cycle of self-doubt and insecurity that prevents us from pursuing our dreams or expressing ourselves authentically. This belief can isolate us, making us feel unworthy of connection or support from others.

Here's the truth: thinking that you have no value can stop you from growing, maximizing your full potential, discovering who you really are, and stepping into the purpose of your calling. When you believe you have no value, you become reluctant to take risks, share your ideas, or engage in meaningful relationships. You overlook the treasure you carry, the gifts and skills you have that can enhance not only your life but the lives of those around you. You might even be sitting on the solution to someone else's problems, but you don't see it, and neither do they, because you're not looking at yourself through the lens of your true worth.

So how do you begin to shift this narrative? Start by embracing compassionate self-awareness. Acknowledge your strengths and embrace the beauty in who you are. Begin to see yourself as the valuable asset you truly are. The shift begins in your mind and in the way you speak to yourself. Recognize your worth daily, even if it feels uncomfortable at first. Trust that your value is intrinsic; it's built into who you are, not based on external circumstances.

Most people go through life waiting for others to validate their worth. Maybe you're waiting for someone to tell you that you're valuable, your parents, your spouse, your children, your friends, or your job. You can't rely on others to affirm your worth. It must come from within. No one knows you better than you know yourself, and no one can define your true value except for you.

Your worth is built into your very being. Every day, wake up and remind yourself of this. Don't wait for the "perfect" time or someone else's approval to take action. There is no perfect time. Life doesn't work that way. If you keep waiting for the "right" moment to get out of debt, you might wait forever. Sometimes you just have to burst through the door.

Think about this: How many times have you had a great idea or a vision for your future, but didn't act on it because you immediately thought, "There's no way I can do that"? Waiting for external validation could cause you to miss out on countless opportunities. People don't always see your potential right away, not because they're mean, but because they don't understand your vision. Here's the kicker: It's not their job to see your vision; it's yours.

You have to believe that you can be debt-free first. Don't wait for everything to be perfect before you act. Step out in faith, even when the waves are high. Take your vision by force. It takes boldness and courage to step out when nothing is ideal. Think about the widow. She didn't wait for her circumstances to change or for someone else to give her permission. She took the risk and chose to act, even in the midst of her grief and despair. She gave herself permission to seek help and take control of her life to save her sons.

I believe the widow probably wondered where to go and who to talk to. In those moments of uncertainty, I believe God whispered guidance to her, telling her to go see Elisha, the man of God. Even though the world said there was nothing she could do because her husband owed a debt and had no life insurance, she probably told herself, "I don't care what they said. God will help me." She trusted God's provision and decided to seek help.

The widow's faith in Elisha represents a powerful lesson for us: you don't always know how things will work out, but you must trust the process. The miracle of the oil multiplying was completely unexpected, especially considering her dire financial situation. She wasn't expecting her husband's death to lead to the start of a business, but sometimes, God works in ways we don't understand at first.

Just like the widow, you need to identify your Resources, whatever small assets you currently have. The widow had only a small jar of oil, but she used it. What do you have? What can you offer? Maybe you have a passion for design, and while you may not have every material you need, you can tap into your local community to gather what you need. Perhaps you've always been intrigued by animals and have a gift for communicating with them. Seek out others who share your passion and learn from their experiences. Use community support to help you grow your creativity and make your business ideas flourish.

This story is a beautiful reminder that faith and community support are key to breakthroughs. Even when you don't know how things will work out, remain positive and trust that the right opportunities will present themselves. When you seek help and align yourself with God's direction, unexpected solutions can arise, just as they did for the widow with the oil. Today, we have more resources than ever to help us become debt-free. You don't have to wait for someone else to permit you to believe in yourself. Look in the mirror and know that you deserve another chance, no matter what you've gotten yourself into. Don't wait for someone else's approval. You have something unique to offer this world, and now is the time to start recognizing it.

In this world, it's easy to feel overlooked, especially when comparison robs us of our confidence. You scroll through social media, see what everyone else is doing, and feel like you're not enough. The truth is that you are enough. God didn't make a mistake when He created you. He gave you everything you need to succeed. Nothing was left out. So, shut out the noise. Your worth is not defined by the number of followers you have, someone else's opinion of you, your job title, your bank account, or even your debt. Instead of seeing barriers to getting out of debt, start seeing possibilities. Tap into your strength, face challenges head-on, and recognize the treasure that lies within you. You are worthy of the life you envision. Truly worthy of it. Believe in your values, trust the process, and step boldly into your future.

CHAPTER 3 WORKSHEET: THE OIL IN YOUR HOUSE - UNEARTHING THE GIFTS WITHIN: DISCOVER WHAT GOD PLANTED IN YOU

"The one person we can't see with our own eyes is ourselves."

SECTION 1: Understanding Your Worth

1. How do you currently see yourself?

Write 3 words that describe the way you usually view who you are.

____

____

____

2. What negative thoughts do you catch yourself believing about your value?

(Be honest, bring the hidden thoughts into the light.)

____

____

3. Where do you think these beliefs originated?

(Check all that apply.)

☐ Childhood experiences

☐ Comparison to others

☐ Past failures

☐ Hurtful words from others

☐ Social media

☐ Trauma or rejection

☐ Other: ______________________________

SECTION 2: Replacing Comparison With Truth

4. Who do you often compare yourself to? Why?

____

____

5. What strengths, gifts, or qualities do YOU have that comparison has caused you to ignore or undervalue?

____

____

____

6. Rewrite one comparison thought into a truth statement.

Comparison thought:

"I'm not as ______________ as they are."

Truth statement:

____

SECTION 3: Intrinsic Value Recognition

"Your worth is built-in. It does not depend on circumstances or approval."

7. What do you offer the world that doesn't depend on money, titles, or praise?

(Think: compassion, creativity, leadership, humor, insight, wisdom, encouragement.)

____

____

____

8. What gifts do you have that could actually be the solution to someone else's problem?

____

____

9. Write a simple sentence affirming your intrinsic value:

(Even if you don't fully believe it yet.)

____

____

SECTION 4: Permission to Act

10. What dream, idea, or goal have you been delaying because you're waiting for validation or "the perfect moment"?

____

____

11. Whose approval have you been waiting on (knowingly or unknowingly)?

(Check all that apply.)

☐ Parents

☐ Spouse/partner

☐ Children

☐ Friends

☐ Employer

☐ social media

☐ "People in general"

☐ Myself

☐ God

☐ Other: ____

12. How has waiting for permission slowed you down or cost you opportunities?

SECTION 5: What Do You Have in Your House?

13. List the resources, skills, tools, or assets you already have (like the widow's jar of oil).

____

____

____

____

14. Which one of these could you use THIS WEEK to take a small step toward your goals?

____

____

SECTION 6: Trusting the Process When You Don't See the Outcome

15. Think of a time when you didn't know how something would work out, but it did.

What happened?

____

____

16. What is ONE area in your life right now where God might be asking you to trust Him like the widow trusted Elisha?

____

____

17. What small, obedient step can you take in faith this week?

(Doesn't need to be big, just obedient.)

____

____

SECTION 7: Your Intrinsic Value Declaration

Write this in your own words:

"My value doesn't come from approval, perfection, or comparison. God built value into me from the beginning.

I refuse to wait for permission.

I trust the process, embrace my gifts, and move forward boldly."

18. Rewrite this declaration in a way that feels personal to you:

____

____

____

19. Sign below as a commitment to seeing yourself through the lens of truth:

Signature: ______________________________________

Date: ____

CHAPTER 4

Choosing God's Appointed Path - Learning to discern divine opportunities and right connections

The next essential step is to select your team. In the real world, no one reaches the top alone. You can't climb the ladder of success without a support system. More importantly, you need the right team. This widow had her right team, the prophet Elisha and her sons. Together, they helped pay off her debts and secured her family's future. She went from preparing for death to preparing for life. That's the kind of transformation that a great team can provide. Your team should add value to you, not drain you. They should be assets, not liabilities.

Understanding the different roles people play in your life is very important. There's an old saying that we meet people for a reason or for a season. These different types of relationships shape our journey in unique ways, providing the support, wisdom, or guidance we need at various stages of our lives. People for a reason enter your life to help you through specific situations, to teach you lessons, or to provide support when you need it most. For example, a mentor may com e into your life at a pivotal moment, offering the wisdom and advice you need to navigate a career change. A friend may show up just when you're going through a tough time, offering emotional support and reminding you that you're not alone.

These relationships have lasting impacts that help you grow and evolve. On the other hand, you may meet people for a season, relationships that serve a temporary but important purpose during a particular phase of your life. This could be a friend you make through a common experience, such as going to school together, or a coworker you work with on a temporary project. Understanding these relationships requires acknowledging their significance in your life and valuing what they have to offer.

Remember, your energy plays a significant role in attracting the right people into your life. When you invest in yourself, whether it's through health, personal development, or creative endeavors, you attract people who resonate with those same values. If you prioritize your health through exercise, nutrition, and self-care, you will find yourself surrounded by others who also care about well-being. If you're an artist or creator, sharing your work and collaborating with others will attract new opportunities, inspiration, and a supportive creative community.

A mindful and calm demeanor can attract peace and positive interactions, which is a reflection of the energy you bring into the world. It's crucial to surround yourself with resilient people, those who understand that obstacles are part of the journey, but who remind you that you're bigger than any challenge. They'll remind you that no matter how tough the situation gets, you have what it takes to endure and overcome.

In times of difficulty, you need positive reinforcement and support from people who truly believe in you. Make sure you surround yourself with people who enrich your life and leave a lasting impression. It's time to let them go or gently guide them to stage left if they don't. You are reading this book right now because I followed this exact formula in selecting my team. As Dr. Darius Daniels wisely said, "You don't go as far as your dream; you go as far as your team." So, who's on your team? I can't say who should be, but I can tell you who's on mine. I have mentors, support people, salespeople, and media professionals on my team.

I've learned that I can't do everything by myself. I did a lot on my own when I first started in business. It was overwhelming, exhausting, and far less effective. Now, with my team, I work smarter, not harder, and I can achieve far more.

As you build your team, you must include people who have already been where you want to go. For example, if you want to buy a house, don't seek advice from someone who has never bought one. You need those who have walked the path before you and can offer practical guidance and wisdom.

Checklist for selecting your team:

1. Identify your goals: What are you trying to achieve? Knowing this will help you find the right people who align with your vision.

2. Evaluate your current connections: Look at the people already in your life. Do they add value? Are they helping or hindering your progress?

3. Seek mentors with relevant experience: These are the people who have accomplished what you want to achieve and are willing to share their knowledge and wisdom with you.

4. Build a network of diverse talents: Don't just look for people in your niche; seek out those who possess skills and knowledge in other areas that complement yours. For example, if marketing isn't your strength, find someone who excels in it and can guide you or handle that aspect for you. Don't just look for skill, seek integrity and expertise as well. Surround yourself with people who believe in your vision, who support your growth, and who challenge you to be better.

Remember, your team is not just a group of people; it's a community that helps elevate your dreams and goals. It's time to start building yours. No one reaches the top alone.

CHAPTER 4 WORKSHEET: DISCERNING DIVINE CONNECTIONS & BUILDING YOUR GOD- APPOINTED TEAM

"You don't go as far as your dream; you go as far as your team."

SECTION 1:Understanding Your Current Season

1.What season are you in right now?

(Choose the one that feels most true or write your own.)

☐ Growing

☐ Healing

☐ Building

☐ Transitioning

☐ Learning

☐ Waiting

☐ Reinventing

☐ Other: ______________________________

2. Based on this season, what kind of support do you need MOST right now?

(Examples: accountability, wisdom, emotional support, strategy, skills, connections.)

____

____

____

SECTION 2: People for a Reason vs. People for a Season

3. List 3 people who came into your life for a reason.

(Why were they sent? What did they help you overcome or understand?) Person:

Reason/Purpose: ________________________________

Person: ______________________________________

Reason/Purpose: ________________________________

Person: ______________________________________

Reason/Purpose: ________________________________

4. Now list 3 people who were in your life for only a season.

(What role did they play?)

Person:

Season/Purpose:

Person:

Season/Purpose:

Person:

Season/Purpose:

5. Are any seasonal people still taking up permanent space?

☐ Yes ☐ No If yes, who?

SECTION 3: Your Energy & What You Attract

6. What energy are you currently projecting?

(Check what feels true.)

☐ Calm

☐ Chaotic

☐ Confident

☐ Uncertain

☐ Hopeful

☐ Anxious

☐ Purpose-driven

☐ Drained

☐ Creative

☐ Isolated

☐ Joyful

☐ Overwhelmed

7. What type of people has this energy been attracting into your life?

____

____

____

8. How would you like to show up moving forward so you can attract the right people?

____

____

____

SECTION 4: Evaluating Your Current Circle

9. List the 5 people who influence you MOST right now. Do they add value? If Yes/No, how do they impact you?

1.

2.

3.

4.

5.

10. Which relationships drain you or hold you back?

(Be honest — you don't have to share this with anyone.)

____

____

____

11. Which connections push you to grow, think bigger, or be better?

____

____

____

SECTION 5: Identifying the Gaps on Your Team

12. What are your top 3 goals right now?

____

____

____

13 What type of people do you need to accomplish these goals?

(Example: mentor, marketing person, financial coach, prayer partner, strategist, creative partner.)

____

____

____

14. What skills or support are you missing?

____

____

____

____

SECTION 6: Seeking the RIGHT Mentors & Connections

15. Write down 3 mentors (real or potential) who have already been where you want to go.

(They can be authors, YouTube voices, pastors, coaches, or people you personally know.) Mentor:

Value: ____

Mentor: ____

Value: ____

Mentor: ____

Value: ____

16. What is one step you can take THIS WEEK to connect with or learn from one of them?

Examples: send a message, sign up for a class, buy their book, watch their training, ask a question.

____

____

____

____

SECTION 7: Discernment: Is This Person From God?

17. Evaluate new or current connections with this checklist:

(Check all that apply to a person you're evaluating.)

☐ They bring peace, not confusion

☐ They challenge me, not discourage me

☐ They push me toward purpose, not comfort

☐ They add value, not drama

☐ They help me grow spiritually, mentally, or financially

☐ They have integrity and consistency

☐ They celebrate my wins

☐ They don't drain me emotionally

☐ They show fruits, not just words

☐ They align with my values and goals

18. Based on the checklist, is this a…

☐ Divine connection

☐ Seasonal helper

☐ Purposeful lesson

☐ Someone to release

☐ Someone to love from a distance

☐ Still seeking clarity

SECTION 8: Build Your God-Appointed Team

19. List the people you want on your team moving forward.

(This may be a mix of mentors, supporters, connectors, creatives, or advisors.)

____

____

____

____

____

20. What will each person contribute to your growth or goals?

____

____

____

21. What will YOU contribute to the team?

(Remember: relationships are mutual.)

____

____

____

SECTION 9: Release & Replace

22. Who do you need to lovingly distance yourself from to make room for God-appointed connections?

____

____

____

23. What type of person do you want God to send you in their place?

(Example: someone wise, uplifting, reliable, experienced, and honest.)

____

____

____

SECTION 10: Declaration & Prayer for Divine Connections

24. Write a short prayer asking God to guide you to the right team and right opportunities:

____

____

____

25. Now write your declaration:

"I choose God-appointed connections. I release what drains me and make room for what builds me. I attract wise, purposeful, supportive, and aligned people. My team will take me where my dream cannot go alone."

Rewrite it in your own words below:

____

____

____

____

CHAPTER 5

Crafting Your System - Building with Heavenly Blueprint: Order, Excellence, and Obedience

Systemizing your tasks is essential for staying organized and moving efficiently toward your goals. You need to set up clear systems, a Standard Operating Procedure (SOP), for how you do things. You must have a structure in place so that you aren't scrambling at the last minute. For example, my system is simple: don't call me at the last minute asking, 'Na'Tasha, can you help me with this or that?' If you want to turn things around, you must systemize your tasks. There are so many moving parts in any venture, and you can't handle all of them on your own.

Here's the key: surround yourself with people who excel at the things you're weak at, people who can do what you don't have the time or expertise to do, and those who enjoy doing things you absolutely hate. When you systemize your tasks and delegate effectively, you free yourself to focus on what you do best. Stay tuned in to your mentor, because when they provide you with their final instructions, those guidelines will take you as far as they can, but eventually, you'll need to go even further. This is where having a clear system in place is invaluable.

Systems for risk reduction and money management are also necessary. Effectively delegate, systematize, and outsource. Don't invest your money in things that aren't necessary for your development. For instance, there's a platform called Fiverr that has been an incredible resource for me. Whether you need a flyer design or a logo created, there are experts who can handle it. This allows you to stay focused on what matters most: growing your talent and presenting your gift to the world without the headache of doing it all yourself. When I didn't have much capital, Fiverr was a lifeline. I could get professional work done without burning through my resources.

Now, let's reflect on how the widow tuned in to her teacher and mentor, Elisha. Remember that four-letter word I mentioned earlier? "Then," once Elisha gave her instructions, she followed them to the letter t She had no idea how this would work, but she trusted the process. That's the formula for success. Find someone who has the answer, and then follow their instructions, especially when it doesn't make sense to you.

Following your own advice got you to where you are today, but if you want to go further, you must be open to following new guidance. If your ideas could have gotten you further, you'd already be there. Elisha gave the widow a set of instructions that, from her perspective, must have sounded completely crazy. Can you imagine her knocking on her neighbors' doors, asking, "Do you have any containers I can borrow?" Can you picture her sons running around gathering containers from everyone in the neighborhood, while oil splashed all over the kitchen? The widow had no clue why she was doing it. Meanwhile, the creditors were still knocking at her door, demanding her children. Yet, she trusted the instructions, and she kept going. She didn't question it.

Then, after collecting all the containers, when they ran out, she went back to Elisha. He gave her the final instruction: "Sell the oil, sell your treasure." Notice he didn't say, "Give it away." He told her to sell it, turning her humble offering into a valuable asset.

Can you imagine her sons asking, "Mom, why are we doing this?" And her reply would be, "Because Elisha told us to." You might be thinking, "As soon as I can see the way clearly from here to there, then I'll get started." It's like saying, "I'm going on a road trip from Texas to New York, but I'm not leaving until I can see the New York state line." When do you think I'll get to New York? Never. I'll never get there because I am waiting for a clear path that may never come. You're waiting for certainty, but the truth is, you can't know how things will unfold until you take the first step.

The reality is, you will never see the full picture before you start. You have to trust that the journey will reveal itself. It's like the widow. She didn't need to know the entire plan before taking action.

She didn't question Elisha. Instead, she trusted the process even when it didn't make sense, even when the creditors were still knocking at her door. She took one step at a time, and that faith led her to the breakthrough she needed.

You never really know how something will turn out. You may have an idea of how you'd like things to go, and sometimes they work out. When they don't, it's crucial to look for the alternative, to shift your mindset, and ask yourself, "How can I make this work?" Instead of giving up, ask how you can turn the situation around.

If you've been waiting for clarity before acting, that's likely what has been holding you back. Just like the widow, you need to take action based on the guidance you've received, even when it doesn't make sense. She didn't stop to ask, "How is this going to work?" She trusted her instinct, walked by faith, and most of all, trusted God. She knew that even when her husband was alive, God had taken care of her and her children, and he would continue to do so.

Trust the process. Follow the instructions. Take the first step even when you can't see the entire journey.

CHAPTER 5 WORKSHEET: CRAFTING YOUR SYSTEM, FOLLOWING INSTRUCTIONS & TAKING ACTION

"Trust the process. Follow the instructions. Take the first step even when you can't see the whole journey."

SECTION 1: Your Current Systems

1. What tasks in your life or business feel chaotic, last-minute, or unorganized? (List at least 5)

____

____

____

____

____

2. Which of these tasks could be solved with a simple system (SOP)? Describe what that system might look like.

____

____

____

____

SECTION 2: Delegate & Systemize

3. What are the top 3 things you hate doing, don't have time for, or aren't good at?

____

____

____

4. List people or resources who can handle these tasks for you.

(Examples: assistants, freelancers, Fiverr, mentors, automation tools)

____

____

____

5. What task will you delegate FIRST this week? Why?

____

____

____

SECTION 3: Your Money & Risk Systems

6. What financial system do you currently have in place? (Budget, envelopes, apps, tracking, none, etc.)

____

____

7. What system needs to be created or improved?

____

____

____

8. What financial tasks should you stop spending money on because they are not essential to your growth?

____

____

____

____

SECTION 4: Following Instructions & Trusting the Process

9. Think of a time when following your own advice kept you stuck. Describe it.

____

____

____

10. What new instruction, advice, or mentorship have you been resisting—even though you KNOW it would help you?

____

____

____

11. What "containers" (opportunities, resources, open doors) is God asking you to gather right now—just like the widow? List them.

____

____

____

____

____

____

SECTION 5: Your First Step

12. What is one action you've been putting off because you were waiting for more clarity?

____

13. What FIRST step will you take THIS WEEK, even if the whole path is not clear yet?

____

____

14. What scripture or affirmation will you stand on as you take that step?

____

____

____

SECTION 6: Reflection

15. After reading this chapter, complete the sentence:

"I will trust the process by…"

____

____

"I will systemize my tasks by…"

____

____

"I will take action even when it doesn't make sense by…"

____

____

CHAPTER 6

Go Sell. Go Pay. Go Live- Turn Your Oil into Income to Pay Down Debt

Many of you are stuck, and one of the reasons is that you haven't yet learned the art of selling. It's time to sell your treasure to sell the oil. You possess gifts, resources, and skills. Go sell the oil; those very things are your treasure. Elisha told the widow to go and sell her treasure, then pay off her debt.

Here's the plan: borrow what you don't have, create what you need, and sell. What do you have? Then, once you sell your treasure, use the proceeds to pay off the debts you owe. Take, for example, if you max out your credit card monthly. What if you sold your treasure? For instance, if people rave about your cooking or desserts, why not turn that into a business? Offer to bake for an event, be it a birthday party, a neighborhood gathering, or a family celebration. Instead of sending them to the bakery, provide your treasure. Use that money to pay off your bills.

Leverage your debt. Whether it's a credit card or a bank loan, understand this: you can borrow other people's money more cheaply than using your own. That's the key to growing wealth. I learned this from my mentor, who could have bought his office building for two million dollars with his own money, but he chose not to. Instead, he borrowed it from the bank. It was cheaper. He knew that borrowing money to build wealth was a smart move. The key is to let the wealth you create pay off the debt. Some of you are obsessed with becoming debt-free, but being debt- free is still zero. You're only back at square one. You're not building anything.

You can choose to live at zero, but I would rather use borrowed money to create wealth and then let that wealth pay off the debt. Once you've paid your debt, the next step is to sustain your turnaround. Elisha said, "Go sell the oil; pay your debt; live you and your sons on the rest." This isn't just a practical strategy; it's a life-altering principle. Go sell. Go pay. Go live. This formula works. It's not just action; it's a mindset that can shift everything.

Go sell. Go pay. Go live. This isn't just a set of instructions; these words are powerful forces. They influenced the widow, shaped her mindset, and dictated her outcome.

Some of you aren't living because you haven't yet figured out how to pay, and you can't pay because you're not selling. Isn't it fascinating how Elisha told her to go borrow, go home, go pour, and then go sell? Each of those actions was filled with intention. Elisha spoke faith to her, and those words carried power.

When you speak with conviction, you align your language with your vision, and that alignment leads to transformation.

When Elisha told the widow to gather containers, pour the oil, sell it, pay her debts, and live on the rest, he wasn't just giving commands. He was planting a seed of possibility in her life. He was showing her a path forward, a path filled with solutions and opportunities, not obstacles and defeat.

His words inspired her belief and shaped her actions. She began to see success as not just possible but inevitable. The widow made a decision that forever changed her life. To decide is not just to "pick one" option; it means to cut off all other options. "De" means "from," and "cide" means "to cut off." To decide is to sever yourself from every alternative, and when you do, you give yourself the freedom to move forward.

Making a decision is what creates confidence. The root of confidence is "confide", meaning trust. Most people lack confidence because they don't trust themselves. Why? Because they've broken their word to themselves time and time again. Every time you let yourself off the hook, you break your trust in yourself, and that erodes your confidence. By deciding to follow through, this widow began to move toward her goal with clarity and confidence. When you learn how to make decisions, you build trust in yourself, and that trust turns into the confidence needed to become the person who can do the thing you've set out to do.

I, too, had to walk through this process. I learned how to stop choosing and start deciding. When I decided to live in financial abundance, everything changed. God began to open doors for me, and I began to hear His guidance, "Go this way, not that way." When you have faith in words, you're more likely to act with conviction. You begin to trust that your words carry power, and as you align them with your vision, they will shape your path. This widow allowed her teacher, the prophet, to be a tool for creating the life she desired, rather than one she feared. Every time he spoke, he was casting a vote for the kind of life she wanted to live.

Her belief in his words fueled her actions. She acted with conviction, pursued her dreams with confidence, and shaped a future in line with her vision. Confidence is not about having all the answers; it's about trusting that each step you take will lead to a solution. Her confidence was built on small steps and the belief that she had the resilience to keep going.

By demonstrating to yourself that you can manage obstacles, no matter how challenging they may appear, you can develop confidence. The widow stopped worrying about what she lacked. Rather, she concentrated on her capabilities. She moved from fear to action as she came to believe in her own mental strength. The widow's breakthrough didn't come from hiding her struggles; it came when she reached out for help. Don't let fear and doubt isolate you. When you share your struggles, you often find that others can provide the insight or encouragement you need to overcome mental blocks. This widow had a solution right under her nose; the oil in her house had always been there, waiting to be recognized. Her freedom was staring her in the face.

Go pour. Go sell. Go pay. Go live. This is the breakthrough formula. It's a blueprint for success that anyone can follow. As Romans 15:4 reminds us, "The things that were written before were written for our learning, that we, through patience and comfort of the Scriptures, might have hope." It's your turn. Get in the game. You've been exposed to these principles; now put them into action. Don't waste this moment. Take the ball, run with it, and congratulations on advance to those of you who will act on it.

I challenge you to take the baton and run with it. I may sound a little frustrated in my tone, but not with you, with the enemy, who has mentally blocked you from your blessings for far too long. The Enemy can't stop your blessings, but what he can do is block you mentally, keeping you from receiving what's rightfully yours. But now that you know how he works, he can no longer use this tactic against you.

You're ready for victory!

CHAPTER 6 WORKSHEET: "GO SELL. GO PAY. GO LIVE."

Unlocking Your Treasure, Building Confidence, and Taking Action

---

SECTION 1: Identify Your Treasure

1. What is the "oil" in your house?

What skills, talents, resources, or gifts do you currently have that could be turned into income?

____

____

____

____

____

2. Which of these do people always compliment you on or request from you?

(Be honest, your treasure is often something you overlook.)

____

____

____

SECTION 2:Create, Borrow, Sell

3. List one thing you don't currently have that you need to borrow or source (tools, knowledge, equipment, funding, help, etc.).

____

____

____

____

4. What can you create this month using what you already have?

(Example: baked goods, a digital service, childcare help, cleaning, writing, décor, consulting, crafts, music, etc.)

____

____

5. What will you sell FIRST? Why did you choose this one?

____

____

____

SECTION 3: Leverage Resources Wisely

6. What debt or credit resource could you leverage, not to buy things, but to create wealth?

____

____

7. How can you use what you borrow to multiply money instead of decreasing it?

(Example: borrowing for equipment, ingredients, marketing, supplies, etc.)

____

____

SECTION 4: Go Sell → Go Pay → Go Live

8. Describe your current relationship with debt. Are you avoiding it, fearful of it, or using it strategically?

____

____

9. What debt will you pay off FIRST with the money from your treasure?

List the exact debt, balance, and your payment plan based on selling your gift.

Debt to Pay: ____________________________________

Amount: ____

I plan to use sales income:

____

10. After paying the debt, what will "living on the rest" look like for you and your family?

____

____

____

Describe your new lifestyle, peace, and stability.

SECTION 5: Decision, Trust & Confidence

11. What major decision are you finally ready to make today?

(Remember: To decide means to cut off all other options.)

____

____

12. In what ways have you previously broken trust with yourself?

(Examples: procrastination, making excuses, starting/stopping projects)

____

____

13. How will you rebuild that trust? List 3 ways.

____

____

____

____

SECTION 6:Shift From Fear to Action

14. What fear or mental block has been stopping you from selling your treasure?

____

15. What truth will you replace that fear with?

(Example: "My gift makes room for me.")

____

16. What is one small action you will take in the next 24 hours?

This action should prove to yourself that you are ready.

SECTION 7: Speak With Conviction

17. What empowering statement will you speak over your life this week?

This should align your words with your vision.

SECTION 8: Your Breakthrough Plan

18. Fill in this powerful formula with your own answers:

GO POUR:

What will you start producing with what you already have?

GO SELL:

Who will be your first 3 customers?

____

____

____

GO PAY:

Which debt will you attack first?

____

GO LIVE:

What will freedom look like for you?

____

____

SECTION 9: Final Reflection

19. What was the widow's biggest turning pointand what is yours?

____

____

20. After reading this chapter, complete this sentence: "I am ready for victory because…"

____

____

____

____

CHAPTER 7

Surrendering Debt - Releasing Burdens, Receiving Freedom: Trusting God to break financial, emotional, and spiritual debt

Most people experience frustration, irritation, worry, anger, sadness, and sometimes even depression when faced with debt. It's amazing how many people find themselves imprisoned by their emotions, held hostage by anxiety and fear about money. I know this from firsthand experience; financial pressure can be overwhelming. It leads to fear of judgment, impaired decision-making, and, in some cases, even negatively impacts relationships.

Debt can cause a deep sense of helplessness, making it hard to see any way out. Believe it or not, debt can even lead to depression and insomnia. But here's something that should bring you relief: You were born with an innate creativity to make money. There's a formula for eliminating the anxiety and stepping into joy even in the midst of your debt journey.

One of the most interesting passages in Scripture is found in Philippians 4:4 says, "Rejoice in the Lord always; and again, I say, 'Rejoice.'" Let that sink in. "Rejoice in the Lord always." And again, "Rejoice." The prefix "re" means to do something again. So, when it says, "Rejoice in the Lord," it means "again, find joy in the Lord." But when? Always. And again, I say, "Rejoice." That's a lot of joy! Here's how I interpret this: As followers of Christ, we've placed our trust in Him as the restorer of our relationship with God. This should lead us to live in a perpetual state of joy, but the opposite is the case for most people.

Too many people walk around with enough anxiety in their souls to sell it by the pound and become millionaires. They're weighed down by worries about what's coming next, which robs them of their present joy. But here's the good news: if God is telling us to live in perpetual joy, it means He has already equipped us to do it. God never tells us to do something we're incapable of doing.

He blessed us with the ability to get out of debt even before we thought about it. He gave us the capacity before He gave the command. If God is telling us to do something, then it is possible. It's within reach.

So, when Scripture says, "Rejoice in the Lord always," it's not a command that's impossible to fulfill. But it's not something we can just conjure up, either. This isn't a joy based on our circumstances; it's not happiness.

Happiness depends on what's happening around us. It's externally driven. Think about the word "circumstance." It comes from "circle" and "stance." Circumstances are the things surrounding us when we stand still; however, when we move, when we take action, those circumstances no longer hold us.

Joy, on the other hand, is an interior state. It's an inside job. Joy comes from awareness, not external factors. People often say, "Wow, Na'Tasha, you're such a positive person! Have you always been this way?" I tell them, "I'm not positive. I'm just aware."

What do I mean? Well, when I woke up this morning, I knew how to get out of bed, but I didn't make myself wake up. God did that. Some people went to bed last night and didn't wake up this morning. That's a gift. I can make myself look, but I didn't make myself see. I can hear the birds outside, but I didn't make myself hear them. I'm aware of all these gifts, and I have joy simply by recognizing them.

You have these gifts, too. You're just not always aware of them. You might be so focused on the debt that opposes you that you miss all the things that are for you. Remember the story of David and Goliath? Saul and his army were more aware of Goliath. David, on the other hand, was more aware of God, who was much bigger than Goliath. When David heard Goliath cursing the armies of Israel, he immediately knew that Goliath, this uncircumcised Philistine, could not defeat him. David didn't back down. He knew his victory was already secured because of the power of God.

The Scriptures tell us that we are more than conquerors. You are better than victorious. You are not just a winner; you are already victorious. It's not "one day I'll be debt-free," but "I'm already debt-free. I'm winning right now." Even in the midst of your financial struggle, you're winning. Even if you're still living paycheck to paycheck, you're still living. Even if you only received one business contract last month, you have a business. Even if you sold only one product, someone saw value in what you offer. You are always winning, because while we see a moving picture of time, God sees a snapshot of eternity.

After the two most potent words in the world, "I am," we need to be extremely deliberate about what we say. Sayings like "I am broke" or "I am stupid" give our limitations eternal power. You can't afford to do that. You have to speak for yourself. You have to talk yourself out of your predicament. Proverbs 18:21 "Death and life are in the power of the tongue: and they that love it shall eat the fruit thereof." When you understand who you are based on whose you are, you'll stop allowing obstacles to feel bigger than you. Debt is not bigger than you. In Philippians 4:4, it says, "Rejoice in the Lord always." How? The very next verse tells us how: "Let your moderation and self-control be known to all men, for the Lord is at hand."

This is where joy meets self-discipline. Self-control doesn't just mean managing your actions; it means being aware of the Lord's presence in every moment. In the presence of debt, the Lord is at hand. When your bank account is empty, the Lord is at hand. When you feel overwhelmed by circumstances, the Lord is at hand.

The joy you seek isn't about pretending everything is fine; it's about choosing to be aware of God's presence in every moment, even in the midst of your struggles. The peace of God, which surpasses all understanding, will guard your heart and mind in Christ Jesus (Philippians 4:7).

This peace will come as you practice His presence, becoming more aware of His presence than your financial difficulties. Even when debt is real, His peace is greater. Even when heartache is real, His joy is more real.

I want you to know that the pain you feel in your financial struggle, the frustration and despair, is real. But God's peace and joy are more real, and they surpass all understanding. They will guide you through this season. When you align yourself with His Word, you'll experience transformation. Trust God, take action, and watch your life shift.

Now, I challenge you to take the first step towards transformation. Join me and Dr. Myron Golden (one of my mentors) in discovering the business that's already inside you, waiting to free you from debt. It's time for you to live a life of joy and freedom. Let's get started!

Ready for transformation? Visit www.bullschallenge.com

CHAPTER 7 WORKSHEET: "Rejoice. Be Aware. Rise Above the Debt."

Mastering Your Emotions, Reclaiming Your Joy & Stepping Into Victory

SECTION 1: Emotional Check-In

1. Which emotions have you felt because of debt?

(Check all that apply)

☐ Fear

☐ Worry

☐ Anxiety

☐ Frustration

☐ Anger

☐ Shame

☐ Sadness

☐ Hopelessness

☐ Depression

☐ Isolation

☐ Other: ______________________________

2. Describe a recent moment when debt made you feel emotionally overwhelmed.

____

____

3. What physical or mental symptoms have you experienced during financial stress?

(Examples: insomnia, headaches, avoidance, fatigue)

____

____

SECTION 2:Awareness Brings Joy

4. List 5 gifts God has given you that you often overlook.

(Think: life, breath, skills, opportunities, provision, people)

____

____

____

____

____

5. List 3 things you became aware of today that reminded you of God's presence.

(These should be small but powerful.)

____

____

____

6. Which circumstances have been distracting you from joy?

(What have you been giving too much power to?)

____

____

SECTION 3: Shift from Circumstance to Awareness

7. Reflect on this truth:

"Circumstances surround me, but they cannot control me when I move."

Where in your life do you need to take action instead of standing still?

____

____

8. What area of your life needs a shift from fear-awareness to God-awareness?

____

____

____

SECTION 4: Your Identity & Your Words

9. What harmful "I am" statements have you been speaking over yourself?

(Be honest.)

____

10. Replace each one with a life-giving "I am" statement rooted in Scripture. Negative "I am" → New "I am"

SECTION 5: You Are Already Winning

11. What wins have you overlooked because they felt small?

(List at least 5.)

12. How does knowing you are "more than a conqueror" shift the way you view your debt?

____

____

____

SECTION 6: Practicing God's Presence

13. In what situations do you forget that "the Lord is at hand"?

(Examples: opening bills, checking the bank app, talking with creditors)

____

14. What daily practice will you begin to stay aware of God's presence?

(Check one or add your own)

☐ Morning gratitude list

☐ Prayer before financial tasks

☐ Daily Scripture meditation

☐ Quiet reflection time

☐ Worship during stress

☐ Declaring "I am" statements

☐ Other: ____

SECTION 7: Peace Beyond Understanding

15. In what situation in your finances do you need God's peace to guard your heart and mind?

____

____

____

16. How will you respond differently this time—with joy, awareness, and trust?

____

____

SECTION 8: Action Steps Toward Transformation

17. What is the FIRST step you will take toward financial transformation this week?

____

18. What gift, skill, business idea, or opportunity has God already placed inside you that you will begin to act on?

____

____

19. What support, mentorship, or guidance do you need to stay consistent?

____

____

SECTION 9: Final Reflection

20. Complete the following statement:

“My joy is not based on my circumstances; it is based on my awareness that…”

____

____

"I am ready for transformation because…"

____

____

www.bullschallenge.com

www.ingramcontent.com/pod-product-compliance
Lightning Source LLC
LaVergne TN
LVHW050917210926
848482LV00012B/476

* 9 7 9 8 3 4 9 6 9 6 0 1 5 *